T0402932

WOEFUL WARS

by Hermione Redshaw

BEARPORT
PUBLISHING

Minneapolis, Minnesota

Credits

Images are courtesy of Shutterstock.com. With thanks to Getty Images, Thinkstock Photo, and iStockphoto. Front Cover – NotionPic, Stasia04, Everett Collection, Ekaterina Bykova. 4–5 – kamomeen, zef art, VikiVector. 6–7 – Hervé Champollion / akg-images. 8–9 – jorisvo, Vectors Bang. 10–11 – Gabi8o, delcarmat, Nicoleta Ionescu, Fotokon. 12–13 – Nancy Bauer, Everett Collection, Steven Hodel, S_O_Va. 14–15– Sammy33, Massimo Todaro, Vuk Kostic. 16–17 – Steve Walker Photography, oculo. 20–21 – rahalarts. 22–23 – Thomas Wyness, Luis Alberto Penaramos. 24–25 – SexyMandalaMan, Adwo. 26–27 – TownFox, Jackie Babe, Anan Kaewkhammul. 28–29 – A.Davey, CC BY 2.0, via Wikimedia Commons,yiannisscheidt. 30 – zef

Bearport Publishing Company Product Development Team

President: Jen Jenson; Director of Product Development: Spencer Brinker; Managing Editor: Allison Juda; Associate Editor: Naomi Reich; Associate Editor: Tiana Tran; Senior Designer: Colin O'Dea; Associate Designer: Elena Klinkner; Associate Designer: Kayla Eggert; Product Development Specialist: Anita Stasson

Library of Congress Cataloging-in-Publication Data

Names: Redshaw, Hermione, 1998- author.
Title: Woeful wars / by Hermione Redshaw.
Description: Minneapolis, Minnesota : Bearport Publishing Company, [2024] | Series: Hideous history | "North American adaptations." | Includes bibliographical references and index.
Identifiers: LCCN 2023010547 (print) | LCCN 2023010548 (ebook) | ISBN 9798888220252 (hardcover) | ISBN 9798888222157 (paperback) | ISBN 9798888223406 (ebook)
Subjects: LCSH: Battles--Juvenile literature. | Military history--Juvenile literature. | Military art and science--History--Juvenile literature.
Classification: LCC D25 .R355 2024 (print) | LCC D25 (ebook) | DDC 355.409--dc23/eng/20230307
LC record available at https://lccn.loc.gov/2023010547
LC ebook record available at https://lccn.loc.gov/2023010548

For more information, write to Bearport Publishing, 5357 Penn Avenue South, Minneapolis, MN 55419.

CONTENTS

PIECES OF THE PAST

There are secrets hidden everywhere. You just need to know where to look. Clues to the past might be buried under your feet right now.

The past was hard for those who had to live through it.

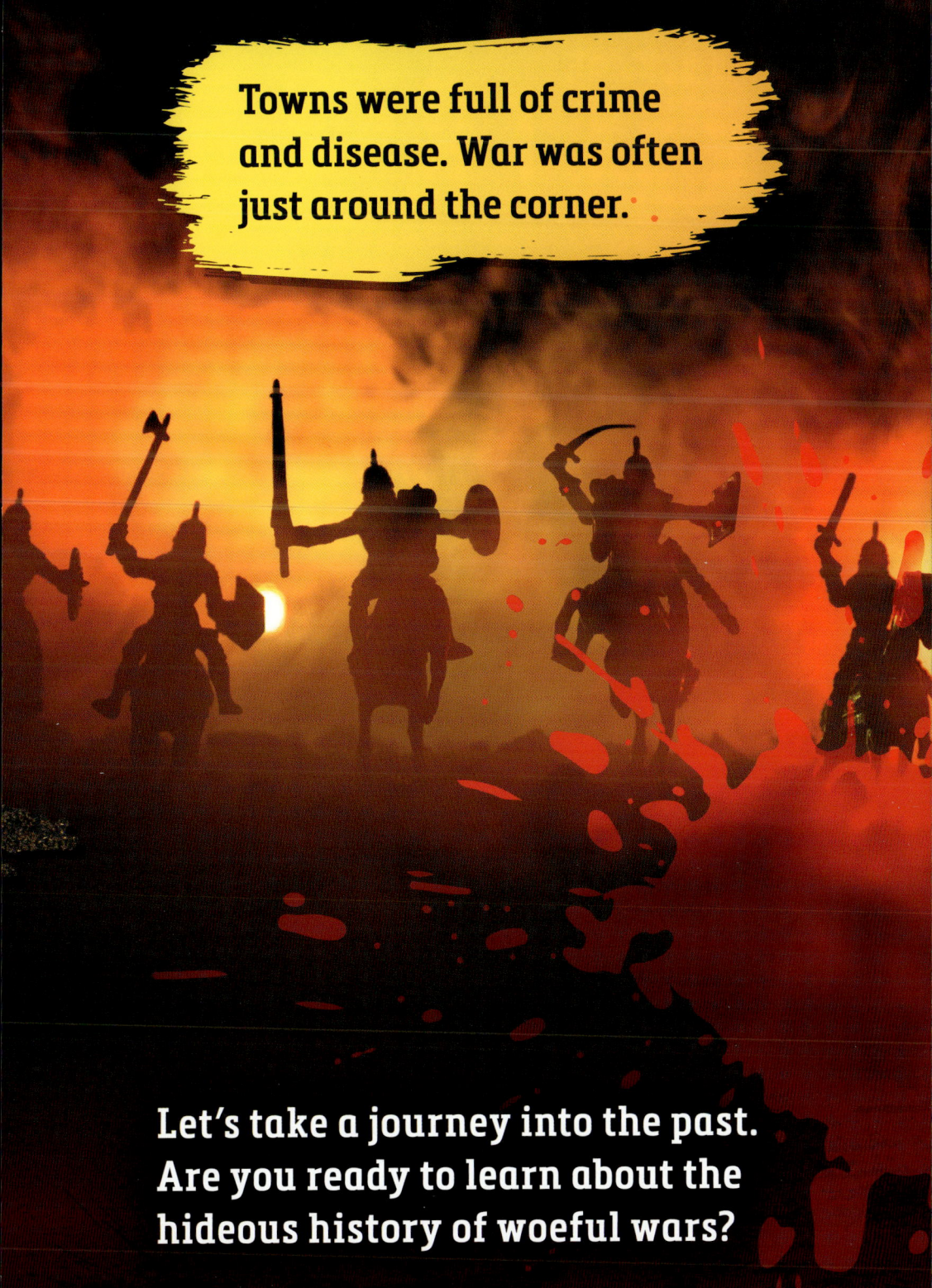

Towns were full of crime and disease. War was often just around the corner.

Let's take a journey into the past. Are you ready to learn about the hideous history of woeful wars?

BATTLE OF TOURS

In 732 CE, there was a large army made up of people called the Moors. They came from Spain and rode their horses through an area of Europe named Gaul.

Their leader, Abdul al-Rahman, wanted the army to take over Europe. Up to that point, it had been pretty easy. That was all about to change.

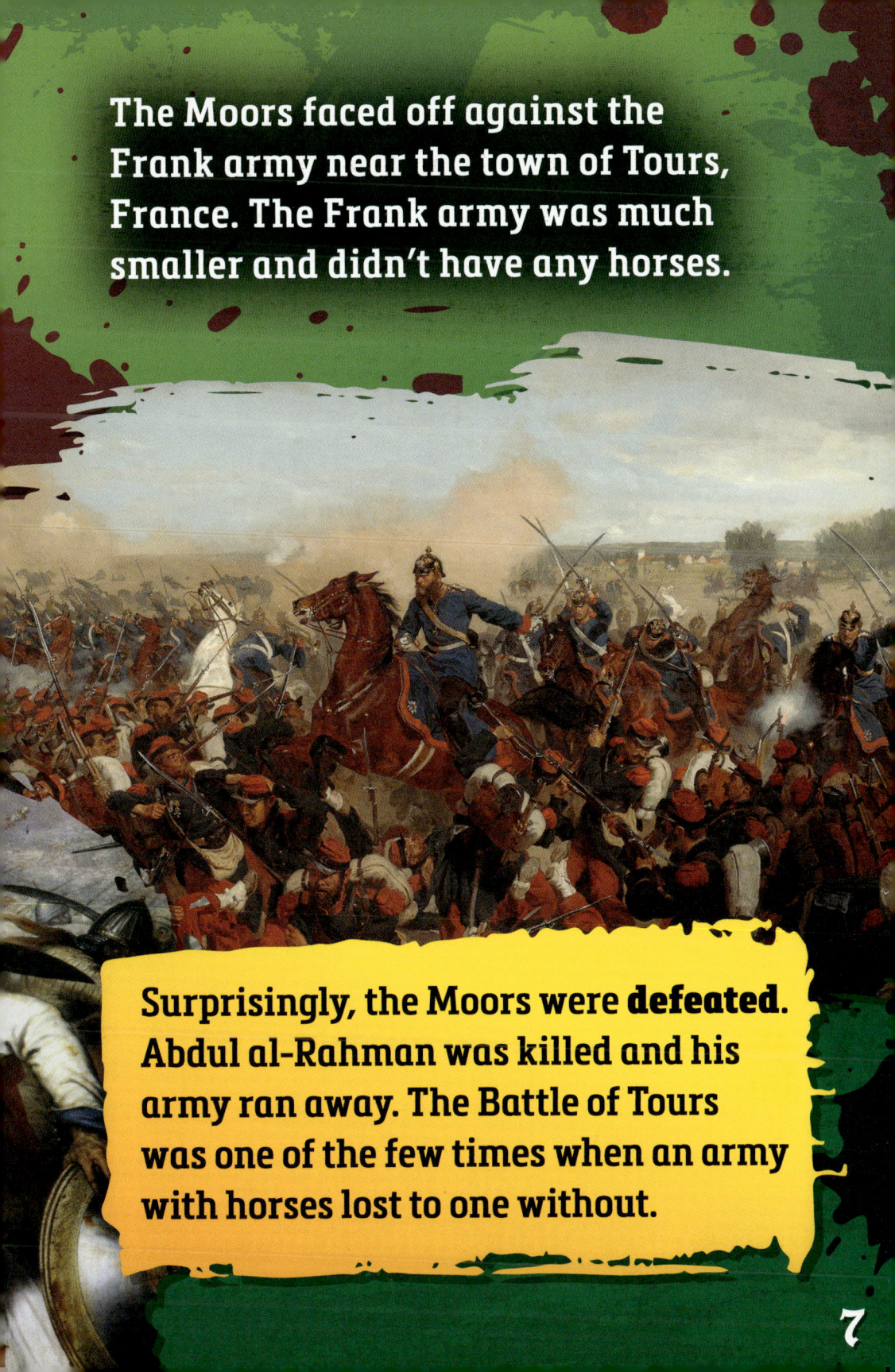

The Moors faced off against the Frank army near the town of Tours, France. The Frank army was much smaller and didn't have any horses.

Surprisingly, the Moors were **defeated**. Abdul al-Rahman was killed and his army ran away. The Battle of Tours was one of the few times when an army with horses lost to one without.

THE BATTLE OF HASTINGS

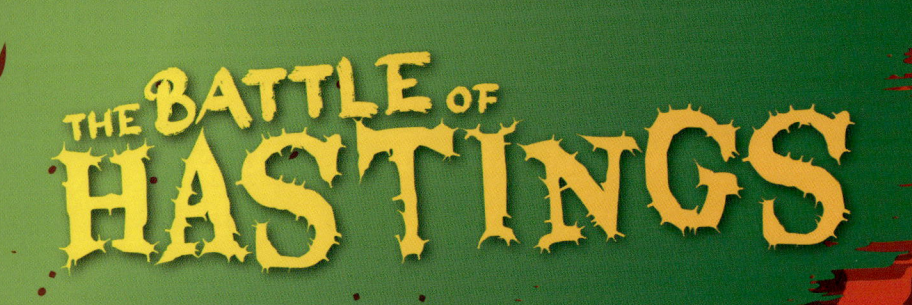

Harold Godwinson was made the king of England in January 1066. He went by King Harold II. However, he wasn't the only one who wanted to be king.

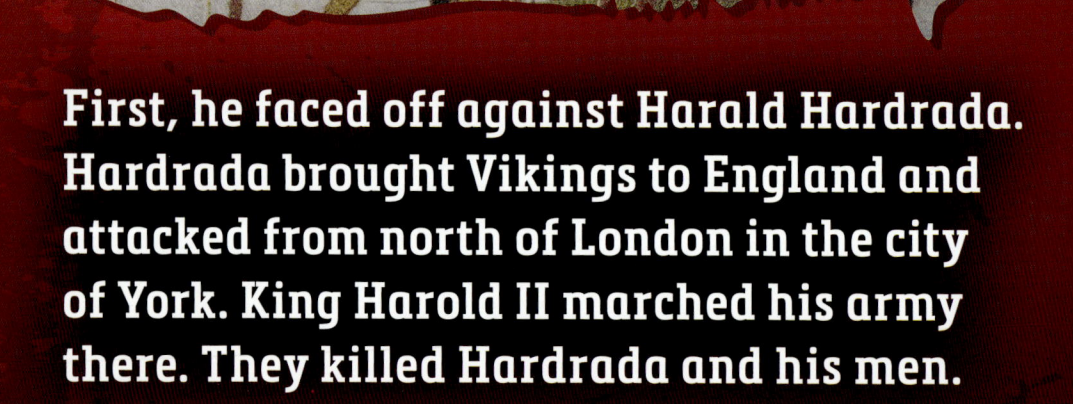

First, he faced off against Harald Hardrada. Hardrada brought Vikings to England and attacked from north of London in the city of York. King Harold II marched his army there. They killed Hardrada and his men.

Then, King Harold II and his army had to travel to Hastings to fight William of Normandy. The king's soldiers were tired by the time they got there.

William's **cavalry** killed most of Harold's army. It is said that Harold was shot in the eye with an arrow. William was crowned king in December 1066.

A NIGHT ATTACK AT TÂRGOVIȘTE

Vlad the **Impaler** ruled ruled Walachia, an area that is part of modern-day Romania. He did many terrible things. However, nothing compared to his actions in 1462.

Mehmed II ruled the powerful Ottoman Empire. Vlad refused to pay him money. Vlad **invaded** some Ottoman villages and killed everyone.

So, Mehmed's army invaded Walachia. Vlad tried to kill Mehmed in the night, but he was chased away.

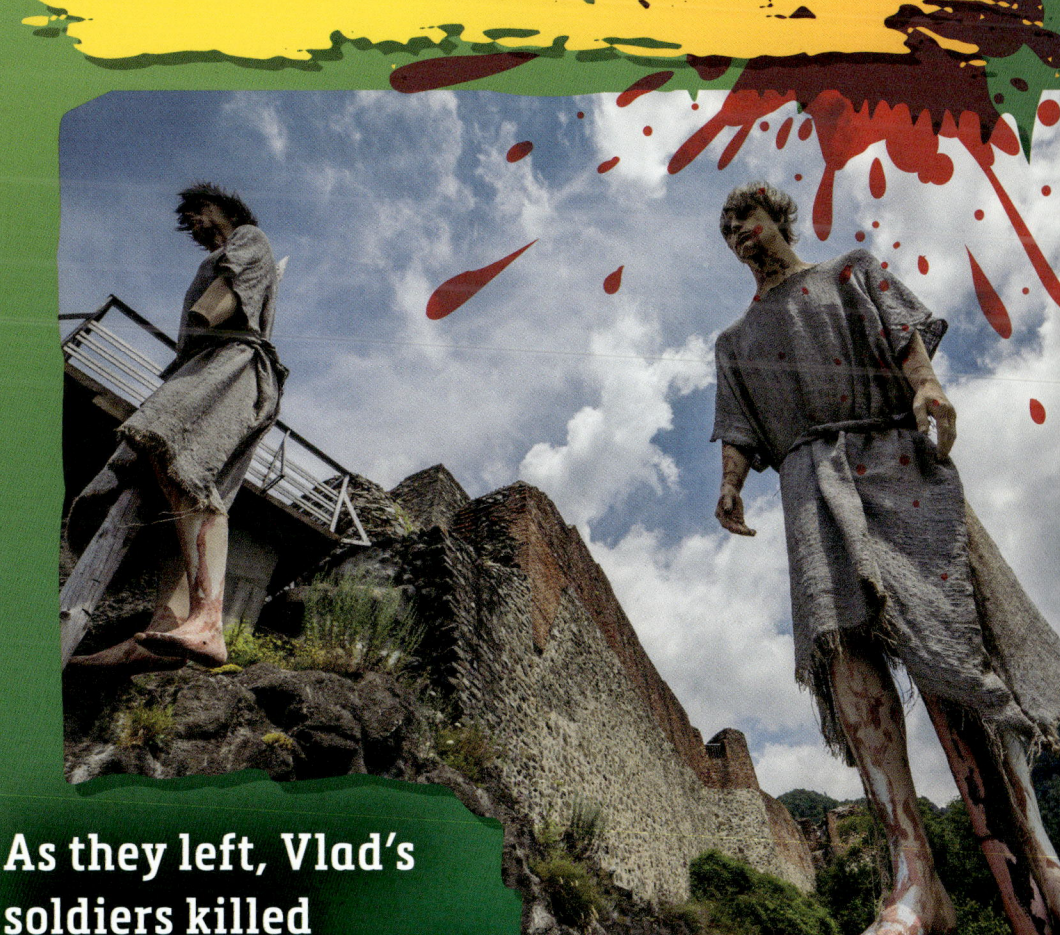

As they left, Vlad's soldiers killed thousands of Ottoman prisoners. They filled a field with the dead bodies on stakes.

These actions gave Vlad the Impaler his name.

THE SIEGE OF ORLEANS

In 1425, a young girl named Joan said she started hearing voices telling her to help the French king and save France.

At the time, England and France were fighting the Hundred Years' War. It had started in 1337, and it looked like England was winning.

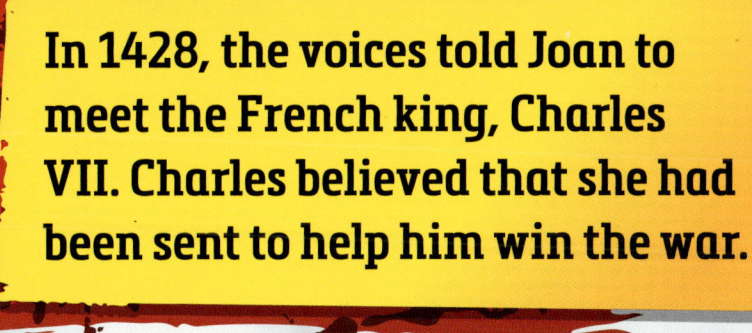

In 1428, the voices told Joan to meet the French king, Charles VII. Charles believed that she had been sent to help him win the war.

Joan of Arc, as she was then known, led an army in Orleans. **Inspired** by Joan's leadership, her army chased the English away.

THE PUNIC WARS

The Punic Wars were fought between the Romans and the Carthaginians. The Carthaginians came from North Africa, but they controlled parts of Spain.

Hannibal became the leader of the Carthaginians. He used his power to follow his boyhood wish of destroying Rome. In 218 BCE, he marched an army toward Italy.

He took his troops through the Alps. Nobody expected them to travel through this huge mountain range. The Romans were caught by surprise.

The Roman army was almost twice as big as Hannibal's. However, Hannibal was a clever general. He managed to trap the Romans. His soldiers killed many of them.

BATTLE OF BRITAIN

In 1940, Winston Churchill thanked the British Air Force for protecting the country.

Never, in the field of human conflict, was so much owed by so many to so few.

The British Air Force fought the German Air Force in the skies over Britain.

The Battle of Britain lasted 112 days. It was the first all-air battle in history. The British were outnumbered. However, they fought off Germany and protected the people of Britain.

Nowadays, the pilots who fought in the Battle of Britain are known as The Few because of Churchill's speech.

THE NAPOLEONIC WARS

One of the greatest war generals in history was a man named Napoleon Bonaparte. In 1799, he ended the French Revolution and became the leader of France.

But France was not done fighting. It soon started the Napoleonic Wars in 1803.

In 1805, Napoleon beat the Austrians and Russians. He gained control over many areas of Europe.

But not even Napoleon could keep on winning. He was finally defeated by the British near the village of Waterloo in 1815.

WORLD WAR ONE

World War I raged from 1914 until 1918. One side included Germany, Austria-Hungary, and Turkey. The other side had France, Great Britain, Russia, Japan, and the United States.

Lots of new **technology** came about during the war. Soldiers used tanks, chemical weapons, and new machine guns.

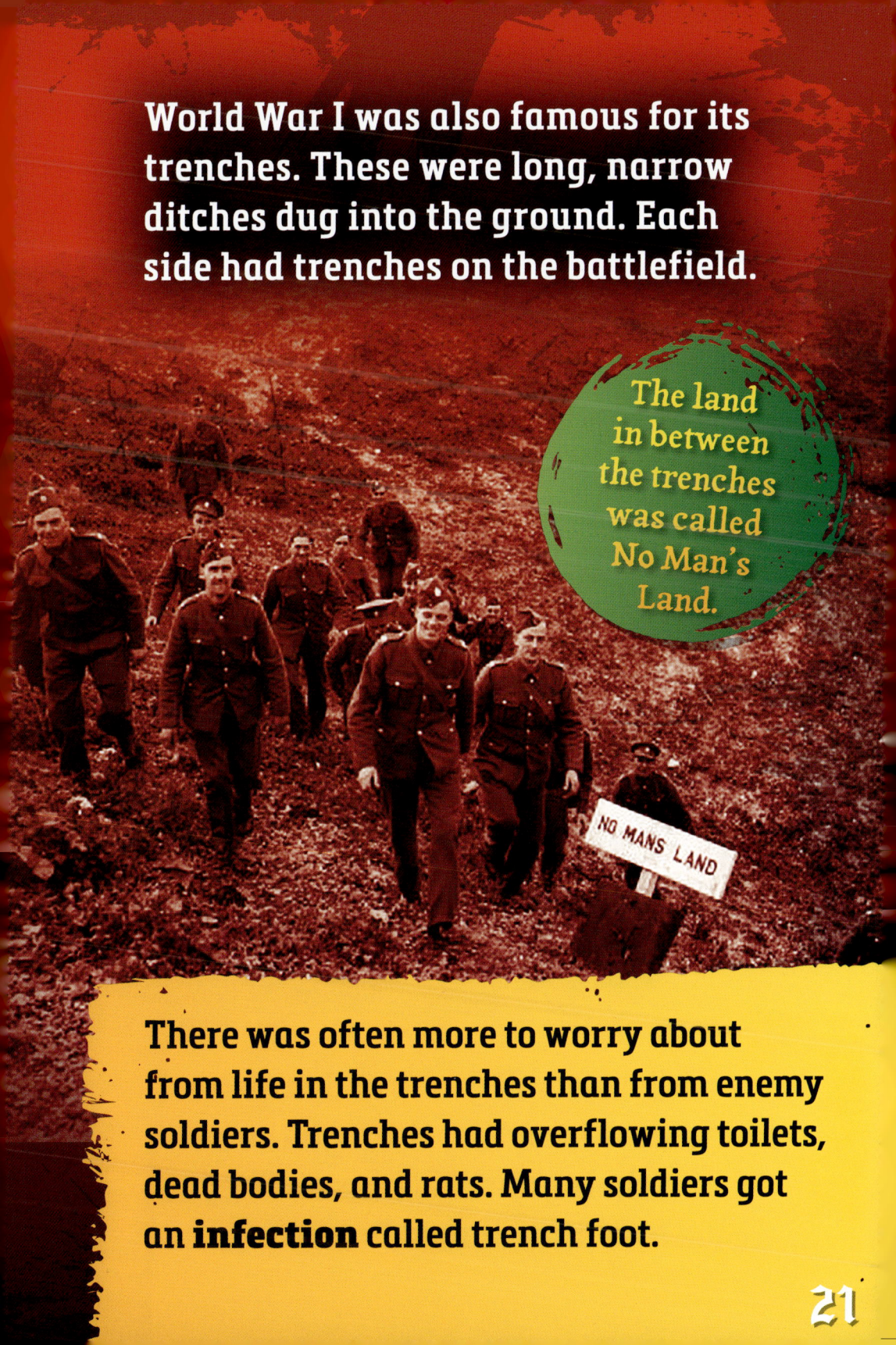

World War I was also famous for its trenches. These were long, narrow ditches dug into the ground. Each side had trenches on the battlefield.

The land in between the trenches was called No Man's Land.

NO MANS LAND

There was often more to worry about from life in the trenches than from enemy soldiers. Trenches had overflowing toilets, dead bodies, and rats. Many soldiers got an **infection** called trench foot.

THE BATTLE OF CAJAMARCA

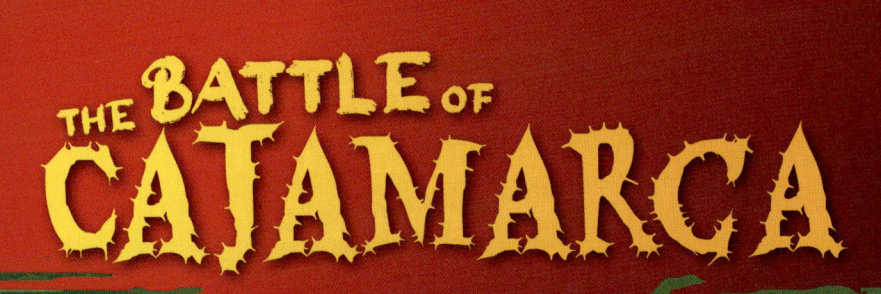

In 1532, Atahualpa became leader of the Incas. He was enjoying his title in the town of Cajamarca in modern-day Peru.

Meanwhile, a small group of Spanish soldiers were traveling through the area with their guns and horses. They were led by a man named Pizarro.

Pizarro and his men formed a plan. Pizarro hid his troops behind buildings and met Atahualpa at the town square.

The Spanish wanted Atahualpa to agree to be ruled by the Spanish king. He refused. So, Pizarro's soldiers opened fire.

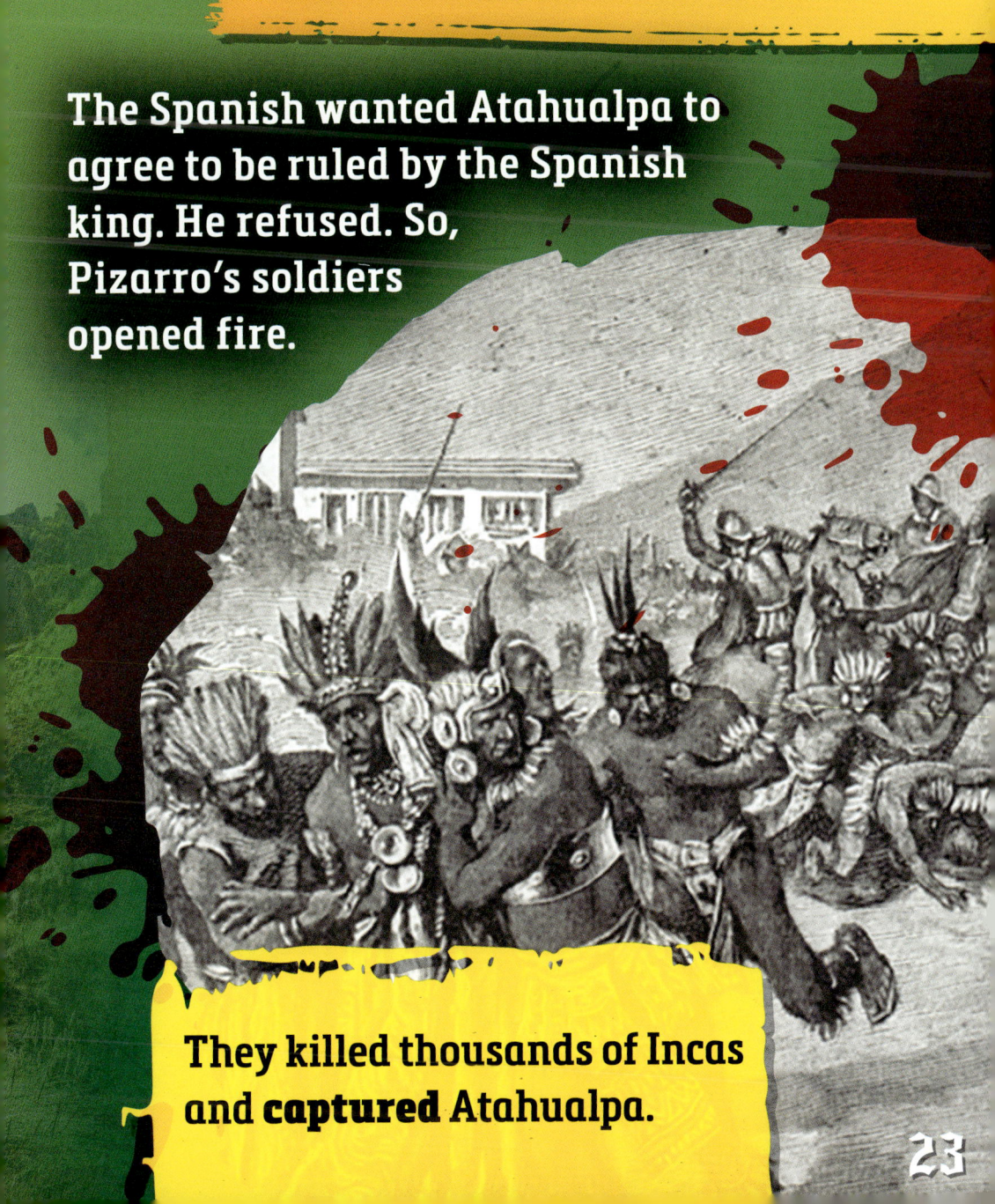

They killed thousands of Incas and **captured** Atahualpa.

THE FRENCH REVOLUTION

Not all wars are between different countries. Sometimes, the people within a country can be at war.

The French Revolution was a fight like this. There were different groups of people in France at the time. Some people were poor peasants. There were also wealthy nobles.

The Revolution started when peasants were tired of being treated so badly. They stormed a **fortress** to steal weapons. They burned down the houses of rich people.

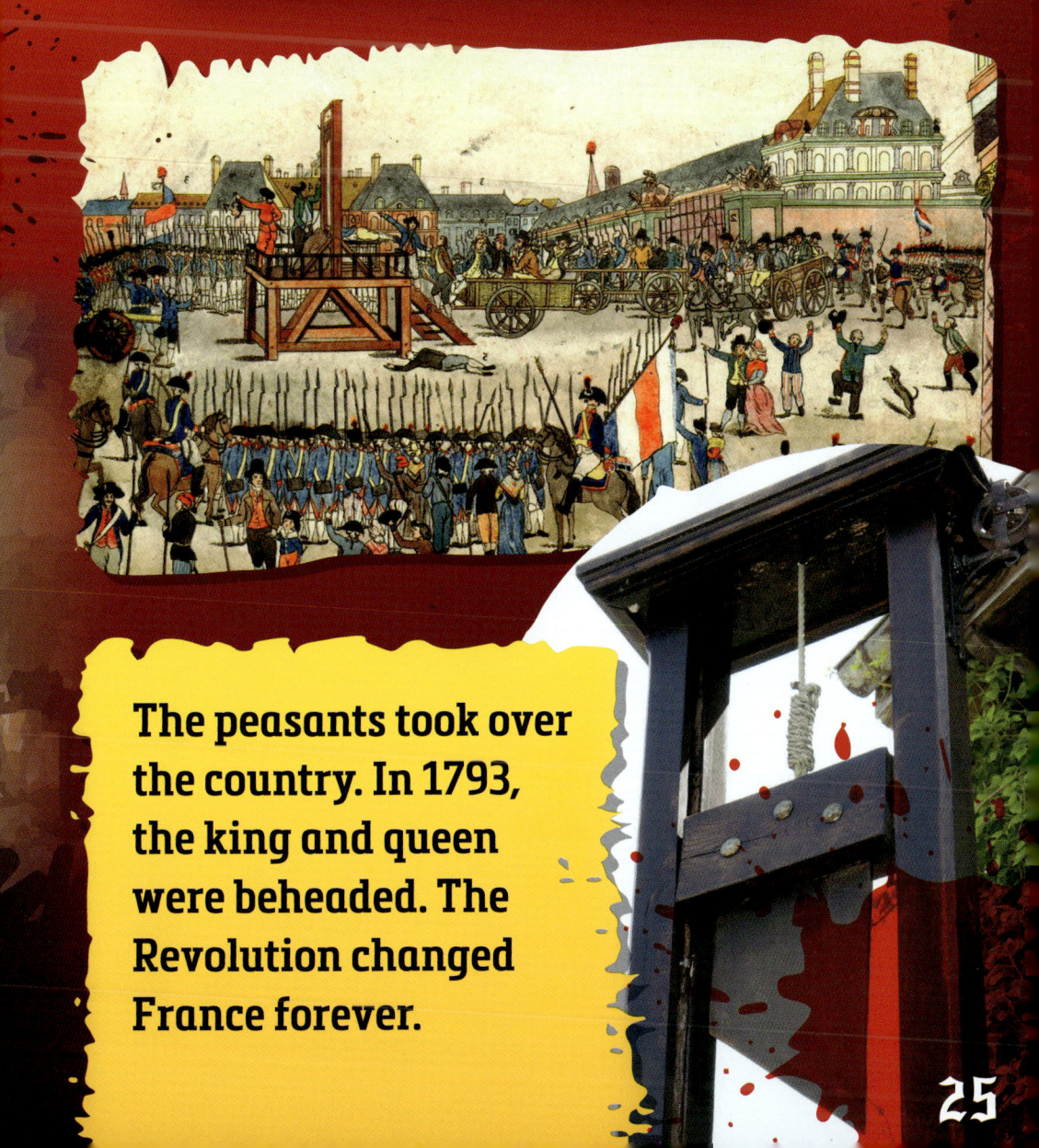

The peasants took over the country. In 1793, the king and queen were beheaded. The Revolution changed France forever.

THE GREAT EMU WAR

After World War I, thousands of Australian soldiers returned home. But many couldn't find jobs. So, the government gave them homes and farms all over the country.

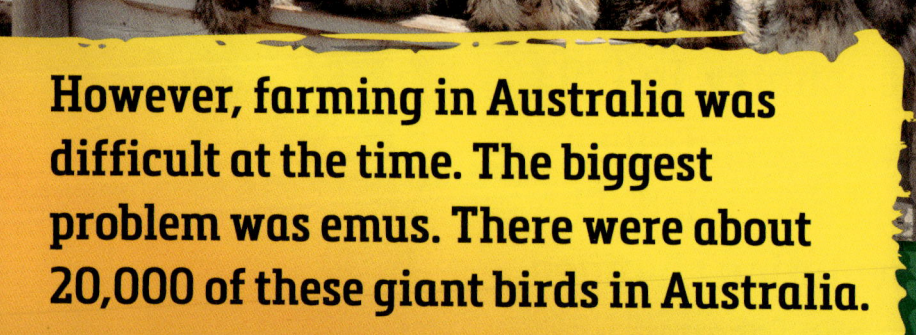

However, farming in Australia was difficult at the time. The biggest problem was emus. There were about 20,000 of these giant birds in Australia.

Emus went wherever they wanted, eating wheat and tearing down fences. The farmers tried to deal with the emus themselves, but the emus were too strong.

It was time to start a war against the birds. The Australians sent a small group of soldiers to kill the birds. However, the battle went badly. The emus won.

27

THE BATTLE OF THERMOPYLAE

In 480 BCE, Persia was huge. It had massive armies. The king of Persia, Xerxes, invaded Greece because he wanted more land. However, the Greeks would not give up their country.

The Greeks were outnumbered by more than 10,000 soldiers. But their leader, Leonidas, knew the best place to fight.

They battled at Thermopylae. This narrow stretch of land was too small for Persia's full army. Their greater numbers would be useless.

The Greeks held their own, and very few were killed. However, a man named Ephialtes betrayed them. He told Xerxes of a secret path that led around Thermopylae.

HIDEOVS HISTORY

Take a deep breath. Allow yourself to calm down. The past was a dreadful place, but it is not where you live now.

Many people met brutal ends during war. These stories showed the horrors of fighting.

GLOSSARY

captured taken during battle

cavalry the parts of an army that serve on horseback

defeated beaten in battle

fortress a large building strengthened against attacks

impaler one who forces pointed objects through things

infection an illness caused by germs getting into the body

inspired created a feeling of belief to do something

invaded entered by force

technology the use of science and engineering to invent useful tools or to solve problems

INDEX

READ MORE

Eboch, M. M. *Living Through World War I (American Culture and Conflict).* Vero Beach, FL: Rourke Educational Media, 2019.

Twiddy, Robin. *A Kid's Life as a Viking (Tough Times to Be a Kid).* Minneapolis: Bearport Publishing Company, 2024.

Vink, Amanda. *The History and Government of Europe (One World).* New York: PowerKids Press, 2021.

LEARN MORE ONLINE

1. Go to **www.factsurfer.com** or scan the QR code below.

2. Enter "**Woeful War**" into the search box.

3. Click on the cover of this book to see a list of websites.